LOOKING BACK

IMPERIAL CHINA

221 B.C. TO A.D. 1294

IMPERIAL CHINA

221 B.C. TO A.D. 1294

HAZEL MARY MARTELL

RSVP

RAINTREE
STECK-VAUGHN
P U B L I S H E R S
A Steck-Vaughn Company

Austin, Texas

Editors: Nicola Barber, Pam Wells
Designer: Neil Sayer
Picture research: Victoria Brooker
Maps: Nick Hawken
Production: Jenny Mulvanny

Consultant: Carol Michaelson, Assistant Keeper,
Department of Oriental Antiquities,
The British Museum, London

Library of Congress Cataloging-in- Publication Data

Martell, Hazel Mary.
Imperial China, 221 B.C. to A.D. 1294 / Hazel Mary Martell.
p.   cm. — (Looking back)
Includes bibliographical references and index.
Summary: A history of China from the time the first emperor
came to power to the death of the Mongol leader, Kublai Khan,
including various aspects of public and domestic life.
ISBN 0–8172–5425–0
1. China — History — 221 B.C.–960 A.D. — Juvenile
literature.   2. China — History — Sung dynasty, 960–1279 —
Juvenile literature.   [1. China — History — 221 B.C.–960 A.D.
2. China — History — Sung dynasty, 960 – 1279.]   I. Title.
II. Series.
DS747.37.M37   1999
951'.01 — dc 21   97-50621
                                             CIP   AC

Acknowledgments

Cover (central image) Werner Forman Archive (background image) Robert Harding Picture Library
Title page Werner Forman Archive **page 6** Dave Brinicombe/Hutchison Library **page 7** (top) Robert
Harding Picture Library (bottom) Elizabeth Weiland/Robert Harding Picture Library **page 9** (top) e.t.
archive (bottom) C. Dodwell/Hutchison Library **page 10** Werner Forman Archive **page 11**
Formosa/Robert Harding Picture Library **page 12** Mansell/Time Inc./Katz Pictures **page 13 and 14**
e.t. archive **page 16** (top) Zhang Shui Cheng/Bridgeman Art Library (bottom) Robert Harding Picture
Library **page 17** Tom Owen Edmunds/Image Bank **page 18 and 20** e.t. archive **page 21** Robert
Harding Picture Library **page 23 and 24** e.t. archive **page 25** Bluett and Sons, London/Bridgeman
Art Library **page 26** Robert Harding Picture Library **page 27** G & P Corrigan/Robert Harding Picture
Library **page 28** e.t. archive **page 29** Werner Forman Archive **page 30** e.t. archive **page 31 and 32**
Werner Forman Archive **page 33** Norma Joseph/Robert Harding Picture Library **page 34** Robert
Harding Picture Library **page 35** e.t. archive **page 36** Sally and Richard Greenhill **page 37, 38
and 39** Robert Harding Picture Library **page 40** Werner Forman Archive **page 41** Robert Harding
Picture Library **page 42 and 43** Werner Forman Archive **page 44** Marc Romanelli/Image Bank
page 45 Robert Harding Picture Library **page 46** School of African and Oriental Studies/Bridgeman
Art Library **page 47** Werner Forman Archive **page 48 and 49** e.t. archive **page 50** Werner Forman
Archive **page 51** Flip Chalfant/Image Bank **page 52** e.t. archive **page 53** Musee Guimet,
Paris/Bridgeman Art Library **page 54** (top and bottom) Robert Harding Picture Library **page 55
and 56** Werner Forman Archive **page 56, 57 and 58** e.t. archive **page 59** (top) Private
Collection/Bridgeman Art Library (bottom) Museo Correr, Venice/Bridgeman Art Library

CONTENTS

INTRODUCTION

Imperial China is the name we give to the period in Chinese history when the country was ruled by an emperor, rather than by a king or a president. It lasted for over 2,000 years, ending in A.D. 1912 when the last emperor was overthrown. In this book, we look back at what happened from the time the first emperor came to power in 221 B.C., to the death of the Mongol leader, Kublai Khan, in A.D. 1294.

THE MIDDLE KINGDOM

The Muztagata Shan mountain range is part of the vast mountainous region in western China.

In ancient times, China was almost completely cut off from the rest of the world. The high mountains, grasslands, and deserts that lie to the north and west, and the vast oceans to the south and east, prevented links from being established with other

civilizations. This remoteness allowed the Chinese people to develop their own ways of life and government with few outside influences. The Chinese called their country Zhong-Guo, which means the "Middle Kingdom." This name reflected their belief that China lay at the middle of the world and was the center of civilization.

The most important outside influence to penetrate China was Buddhism. This religion started in India in the 6th century B.C. Knowledge of the Buddha and his teachings spread to China by about A.D. 100. Buddhism had a considerable impact both on Chinese culture and history.

HOW DO WE KNOW?

Our knowledge of life in ancient and Imperial China comes from many different sources. There are written records on bone and stone, bronze and silk, in addition to paper. There are paintings on silk and on the walls of tombs, showing scenes from everyday life. Many tombs contain pottery models of buildings and people, together with real clothes and weapons, tools, and ornaments. These objects were placed in the tomb for the dead person to use in his or her next life. Archaeologists study these artifacts carefully to work out how they were made, and what they were used for. Sometimes there are remains of food and drink in a tomb. These remains tell us about the kind of diet that was available. Sometimes even the body of the dead person has remained intact. It can be examined to try to discover the cause of death and if the person suffered from any diseases during life. From all this information, archaeologists and historians have built a picture of what life was like thousands of years ago, for both poor and rich people in China.

This figure of a woman was excavated from an early 8th-century tomb. Pottery figures, such as this, give archaeologists information about fashion and clothing, as well as pottery-making techniques.

A CLOSER LOOK

The vast grasslands to the north of China were inhabited by nomadic peoples, such as the Mongols. They lived by herding sheep and cattle. They often attacked China and sometimes managed to invade the country.

A shepherd boy in present-day Mongolia.

CHINA BEFORE THE FIRST EMPEROR

When Qin Shi Huangdi made himself First Emperor of China in 221 B.C., he set up a system of government that hardly changed over the next 2,000 years. However, although he was a powerful man and had a son to succeed him when he died, the dynasty (ruling family) that he founded outlived him by only a few years. There was a brief time of rebellion and chaos before another dynasty became strong enough to take control of the whole country once more. This pattern repeated itself time and time again throughout the period we are looking at in this book, though not all dynasties were as short-lived as that of the Qin. The Chinese used the theory of the Mandate of Heaven to explain why these changes took place, and why one dynasty succeeded another.

THE MANDATE OF HEAVEN

From the time of the earliest kings, Chinese rulers called themselves the Sons of Heaven. They claimed that Heaven had given them its mandate (permission) to rule over the Chinese people. To keep the mandate, each king—and later, each emperor—had to rule well and treat the people fairly. He also had to listen to his advisers and keep peace in the country. In exchange, his people had to obey him. If a king ruled badly and treated the people unfairly, there would be riots and rebellions against him. If the people managed to defeat the king, Heaven would remove its mandate from him because he was no longer fit to rule. The Mandate of Heaven then passed to a new ruler, and a new dynasty came to power.

AN ANCIENT CIVILIZATION

Chinese civilization was already well-established when Qin Shi Huangdi came to power. As early as 6000 B.C., people started to settle down in villages along the Yellow River and farm the fertile land, using tools made from stone, bone, and wood. By 5000 B.C. they knew how to make pottery, and by about 2000 B.C. copper was being mined and worked. Some time after this, weapons and ornaments were being made from bronze, a combination of copper and tin. Meanwhile some families began to emerge as leaders. Gradually these families became more powerful than the rest and began to rule over increasingly large areas. According to legend, by 2100 B.C. one family was powerful enough to rule over most of the country. The name of this family was Xia, and it is said that the Xia dynasty lasted for 600 years. No one knows whether the Xia really existed or not, but there is definite proof that the Shang dynasty came to power around 1500 B.C. It ruled for almost 400 years, before being replaced by the Zhou dynasty.

During the Shang dynasty, skilled metalworkers made large wine vessels out of bronze.

A CLOSER LOOK

The Yellow River gets its name from its color. It often looks yellow because of the yellow-colored soil, called loess, that washes into it during periods of flooding. Its Chinese name is *Huang he.* "Huang" means "yellow," and "he" means "river."

The Yellow River.

The Zhou dynasty lasted from 1050 to 221 B.C. Under the Zhou kings, the land in China was held under the feudal system. This meant that the king owned all the land, but he allowed his noblemen to hold large areas of it in exchange for their promise to protect the land from his enemies and to provide soldiers for him in times of war. In the same way, the noblemen rented plots of land to peasant farmers, who paid for it by service rather than with money. This service could include working on the nobleman's land or going to war if the king needed extra soldiers for his army.

Between the 8th and the 5th centuries B.C., the use of iron tools meant that the production of crops increased, and the noble families became richer. As they became wealthier, these families also became more powerful. From 475 B.C. on they began to fight among themselves for control of the country. At the same time, two sets of ideas came into being which would greatly influence Imperial China from the Han dynasty onward. They were Confucianism and Daoism.

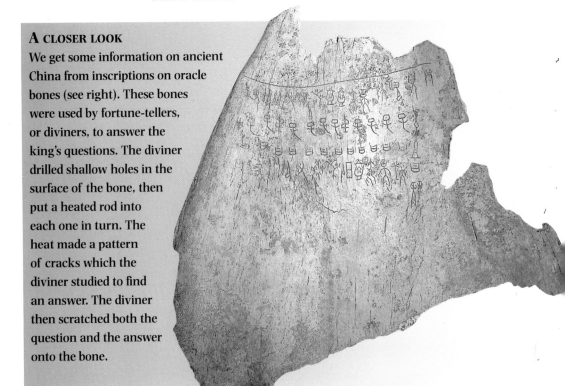

A CLOSER LOOK

We get some information on ancient China from inscriptions on oracle bones (see right). These bones were used by fortune-tellers, or diviners, to answer the king's questions. The diviner drilled shallow holes in the surface of the bone, then put a heated rod into each one in turn. The heat made a pattern of cracks which the diviner studied to find an answer. The diviner then scratched both the question and the answer onto the bone.

Confucius often taught out of doors with his students gathered around him. Among other things, he told them to obey their parents, elders, and rulers. He also taught that wives should obey their husbands.

CONFUCIANISM

Confucianism is a set of ideals to live by, rather than a religion, and it takes its name from the scholar and thinker, Confucius. He was born in China around 551 B.C., just as the country was once more heading toward war and chaos. When Confucius was 22 years old, he became a teacher. He traveled around the country, teaching the sons of noble families. He told his students that people were born good and that they all had a duty toward each other. This duty included kindness, obedience, respect, courage, sympathy, and sincerity. Confucius thought that everyone had a place in society and that they should be content with that place. He also said that people should try and live in peace and harmony with the world around them.

Confucius wanted to change society by persuading rulers to lead good and virtuous lives. He thought that if they did so, their subjects would follow their example. He always hoped for an adviser's post at a nobleman's court, where he could try out some of his ideas. But, although he was greatly revered by his followers, no such appointment came his way. In old age, he returned to his birthplace where he died in 479 B.C. His thoughts and ideas were later written down by his followers.

DAOISM

The beliefs that make up Daoism are about as old as Confucianism. They were developed by several people over a long period of time. According to tradition, one of the major Daoist philosophers, or thinkers, was Lao-tzu, who was said to have worked in the royal library during the Zhou dynasty. Many Daoist ideas are contained in a book called the *Daodejing*, supposedly written by Lao-tzu. Daoists believed that people were just another part of the natural world, along with animals, plants, trees, birds, the sky, and the Earth itself. They emphasized the need for a simple life in which the balance of *yin* and *yang* were very important. (See box on page 13.) In many ways Daoist ideas were the opposite of Confucius's teachings because they stressed the importance of non-action and the need to retire from the business of the world. Daoism is named after *Dao* which means "the Way," the universal path that guides all living things.

According to tradition, Lao-tzu was saddened by people's unwillingness to accept his ideas. He climbed on a water buffalo and set off westward, but he was persuaded to turn back and write the Daodejing.

A CLOSER LOOK

Chinese tradition says that the world is controlled by two great natural forces, *yin* and *yang*. They are both equal but opposite, and should be kept in exact balance with each other, not only in nature, but also in art. Y*in* and *yang* also represent other things that are equal but opposite. For example, *yin* represents females, quietness, darkness, valleys, and the color black, while *yang* represents males, noise, light, hills, and the color white.

Studying the yin-yang *symbol (in the middle of the banner).*

THE RISE OF THE STATE OF QIN

The time between 475 and 221 B.C. in China is called the Warring States period because there were around 200 small states fighting against each other. This number began to decrease as, one after the other, small states were defeated and taken over, and bigger ones began to develop. After around 200 years of warfare, just seven states were left. They were Qi, Chu, Han, Qin, Wei, Yan, and Zhao. The leaders of these states sometimes called themselves kings, but they were still subjects of the Zhou king. However, by 256 B.C. the leader of the state of Qin had managed to take control of the other states, and in 249 B.C. he finally overthrew the Zhou dynasty.

THE QIN DYNASTY

REORGANIZING THE EMPIRE

Qin Shi Huangdi was the first ruler of the Qin dynasty, and, in 221 B.C., he proclaimed himself the First Emperor of China. Under his rule, the organization of government was changed completely. He abolished the feudal system (see page 10) by making the peasants pay taxes directly to him in exchange for their land. This new system took power away from the nobles. So, to prevent rebellions, Qin Shi Huangdi forced perhaps as many as 120,000 nobles and their families to move to his capital at Xianyang. He detained the nobles at his court where he could keep an eye on what they were doing. This tactic also moved the nobles far from any would be supporters on their estates in the country.

Qin Shi Huangdi's chief adviser was Li Si, the man who had encouraged him to take control of the whole of China when he was king of the state of Qin.

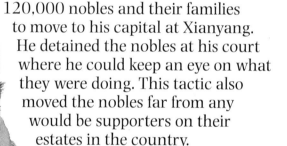

This portrait of Qin Shi Huangdi was painted from the artist's imagination, probably in the 18th century A.D.

14

A CLOSER LOOK

Qin Shi Huangdi's chief adviser, Li Si, believed in a set of ideas called Legalism. Legalism stressed the importance of obedience. People who obeyed the emperor were supposed to be rewarded, and those who broke the emperor's rules punished. In Qin Shi Huangdi's reign, however, there were far more punishments than rewards, including branding, mutilation, hard labor, and execution. Two of Qin Shi Huangdi's own sons even obeyed their father when they were ordered to commit suicide. Legalism also tried to control the way people thought by forbidding them to look back at the past favorably, or to criticize the present.

Together they made plans to unite the country, which had been at war for so long. They started by dividing China into 36 districts, which they called commanderies. Each commandery was administered by a military official, a civil (citizen) official, and an imperial official, all of whom were appointed and paid by the emperor. The military official was responsible for everything to do with the army, including recruiting soldiers and paying them. The civil official dealt with everything relating to the rest of the population, making sure people paid their taxes and obeyed the law. The imperial official was a censor who watched over what everyone was doing and reported his findings directly to the emperor.

This map shows the six states defeated by the state of Qin and the extent of the Qin Empire.

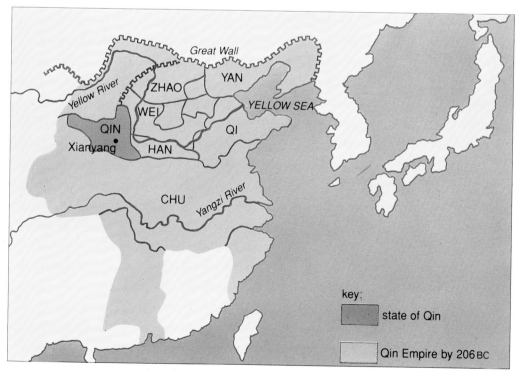

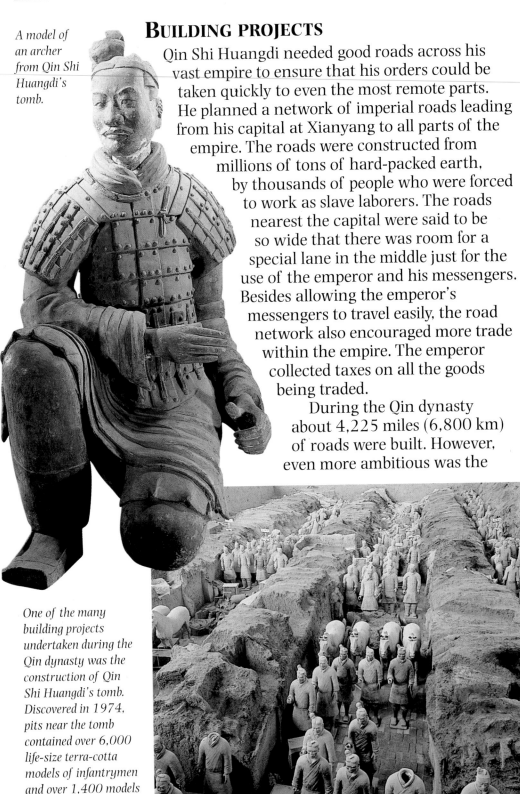

A model of an archer from Qin Shi Huangdi's tomb.

BUILDING PROJECTS

Qin Shi Huangdi needed good roads across his vast empire to ensure that his orders could be taken quickly to even the most remote parts. He planned a network of imperial roads leading from his capital at Xianyang to all parts of the empire. The roads were constructed from millions of tons of hard-packed earth, by thousands of people who were forced to work as slave laborers. The roads nearest the capital were said to be so wide that there was room for a special lane in the middle just for the use of the emperor and his messengers. Besides allowing the emperor's messengers to travel easily, the road network also encouraged more trade within the empire. The emperor collected taxes on all the goods being traded.

During the Qin dynasty about 4,225 miles (6,800 km) of roads were built. However, even more ambitious was the

One of the many building projects undertaken during the Qin dynasty was the construction of Qin Shi Huangdi's tomb. Discovered in 1974, pits near the tomb contained over 6,000 life-size terra-cotta models of infantrymen and over 1,400 models of cavalrymen and their horses.

A large part of the Great Wall of China can still be seen today. It follows the line of Qin Shi Huangdi's wall, but it has been repaired and rebuilt many times over the years, especially in the 15th and 16th centuries.

construction of what we now call the Great Wall of China. Qin Shi Huangdi wanted to protect China from invasion by nomadic peoples. (See page 7.) Some walls had already been built in the north, and Qin Shi Huangdi decided that these should all be joined together and extended to make a continuous wall from the Yellow Sea to central Asia.

With all its twists and turns, the Great Wall then measured about 4,000 miles (6,400 km) and stood about 30 feet (9 m) high. It took about ten years to build, between 214 and 204 B.C. It was constructed from stone and earth. At regular intervals along the wall, there were watchtowers that were about 39 feet (12 m) high. These were used to guard the wall and also to send signals, using smoke by day and fire by night, to the capital at Xianyang. The Great Wall was built by soldiers, convicts, prisoners of war, and slave laborers. Because it was in a remote part of the country, a special network of roads also had to be built to transport workers and supplies, such as tools and food.

17

A CLOSER LOOK

Qin Shi Huangdi did not want the Chinese people to question his methods of government, or to look back to earlier times and think that life was better then. To prevent any criticism of his rule, he ordered the burning of all books except for practical books on medicine, farming, and fortune-telling, and those that praised him. Even discussing the books of Confucius became a crime punishable by death. However, some scholars managed to hide copies of forbidden works, or to memorize passages for future use.

Qin Shi Huangdi orders the burning of books. It is claimed that he also executed many scholars.

STANDARDIZING SYSTEMS

Before 221 B.C., each state in China had its own system of money, writing, weights, and measures, in addition to its own laws and punishments. The First Emperor realized that the country would never be truly united if this continued, and so he decided to standardize everything. He introduced small, circular, bronze coins that had the same value no matter where they were used. This made it much easier for people to trade, since the same money could be used to buy goods anywhere in the country. It also made it easier for government officials to work out how much tax should be paid to the government on all goods being transported to and from the markets.

Qin Shi Huangdi also made everyone use just one system of weights and measures and one form of writing, based on about 3,000 characters. Each of these characters represented an object or an idea, as well as a sound. This meant that people in one region could understand what was written by people from another region, even though they might not be able to understand their spoken words. It also meant that everyone could understand the emperor's orders when they were written down, and so there were no excuses for not obeying him.

QIN SHI HUANGDI'S FEARS

Qin Shi Huangdi's rule was very harsh, but he knew he had to reward people occasionally or they would rebel against him. He gave gifts of houses or money to officials who served him well, and loyal villages were sent a couple of sheep to roast for a feast once a year. In 214 B.C. the emperor even gave a gift of two sheep and some rice to every village in his empire.

In spite of his fears of assassination, Qin Shi Huangdi died of natural causes in 210 B.C. and was succeeded by his son. In addition to being harsh like his father, he was also weak and greedy. Within a year, an army of peasants rose up against him. It was defeated, and its leaders were killed. But new leaders soon came forward, and the rebellion continued. In 206 B.C. the Qin dynasty was conquered by rebels led by Liu Bang. Four years later, Liu Bang became the first emperor of a new dynasty.

A CLOSER LOOK

Qin Shi Huangdi lived in constant fear of being murdered. He was said to sleep in a different room of his palace every night so that would-be killers would not know where to find him. In fact, there were at least three attempts to assassinate him. In 227 B.C. he was attacked by a man with a poisoned dagger that was concealed in a rolled-up map. Then a blind musician tried to hit him with a lead-filled harp! Finally, there was an ambush while he was traveling in one of the provinces, but luckily for the emperor the attackers targeted the wrong carriage.

THE HAN DYNASTY

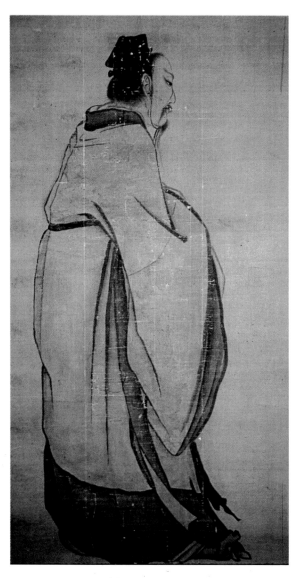

A portrait of the emperor Wudi. His military campaigns greatly expanded the Chinese empire, but he paid for them by increasing taxes and taking control of the production of salt, iron, and wine.

Liu Bang became the first emperor of the Han dynasty in 202 B.C. and made Ch'ang-an (Xi'an or Hsi-an) the new capital of China. He had been brought up as a peasant and probably could neither read nor write. He was less harsh than Qin Shi Huangdi, and did not follow Legalist ideas. (See page 15.) Nevertheless, he managed to reunite the Chinese people and hold the empire together. He and his successors encouraged trade and industry, as well as agriculture, and soon China was flourishing again.

Emperor Wendi, who reigned from 179 to 157 B.C., used Daoist beliefs as the basis for his government, but his grandson, Wudi, adopted Confucian ideals to rule his empire. Wudi reigned from 141 to 87 B.C. He ordered scholars to make new versions of the Confucian books which Qin Shi Huangdi had destroyed, using hidden copies or scholars' memories. Wudi encouraged the study of these books by making them the basis for examinations for the many civil (government) servants and officials who helped him run the country. He started a state education plan in which the main subject was the study of the

The works of Confucius are made up of
five books, known as the "Five Classics,"
plus a sixth book called the *Analects*. The
"Five Classics" are the *Book of Changes*,
the *Book of Documents*, the *Book of
Songs*, the *Book of Rites*, and the *Spring
and Autumn Annals*. They are probably
a collection of writings from Zhou times
that were gathered together by
Confucius. Only the *Analects* contains
Confucius's own words, and these
sayings were written down by his
students after his death.

works of Confucius. He also set
up a university, known as the
Imperial Academy, where all
the professors were experts in
the works of Confucius.

EXPANSION UNDER WUDI

In spite of the Great Wall, nomads
from the north continued to raid
China. In 166 B.C. they came to
within 99 miles (160 km) of the
capital, Ch'ang-an. The early
Han emperors had tried bribing
the nomads with gifts of silk and
rice and offers of marriage to
imperial princesses, but with little success. Wudi
tried different tactics. In 139 B.C. he sent an official,
Zhang Qian, on a journey to lands beyond the
western borders of China. Zhang Qian's orders
were to try to persuade the western nomads to join
with the Chinese in the fight against the nomads
to the north. However, Zhang was held
prisoner for ten years and, after a
courageous escape, returned in
126 B.C. He brought back with him
the first reliable information about
civilizations beyond China, including
news of the cultivation of wheat, and
of grapes for wine, and of the merchants
in Parthia (see map on page 22) who
were importing Chinese silk.
Meanwhile Wudi had sent
300,000 troops on an expedition

*This bronze figure of
a horse dates from the
2nd century A.D.*

A CLOSER LOOK
Zhang Qian brought back news of the
big, strong horses he had seen in Fergana,
today's E. Uzbekistan. Emperor Wudi wanted these horses
to carry his soldiers into battle. In 101 B.C., Chinese troops
captured some of these horses and took large numbers of
them back to China.

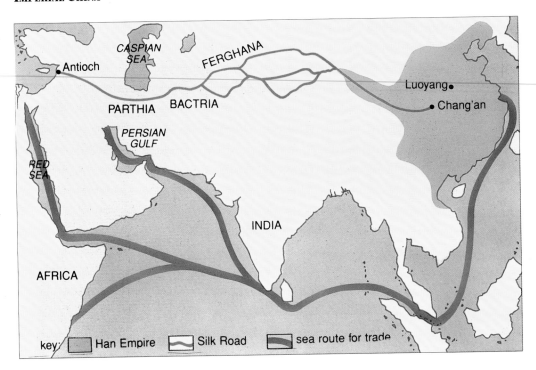

CASPIAN SEA

FERGHANA

Antioch

PARTHIA BACTRIA

Luoyang

Chang'an

PERSIAN GULF

RED SEA

INDIA

AFRICA

key: Han Empire   Silk Road   sea route for trade

This map shows the Silk Road and other trade routes between China and countries to the west, as well as the extent of the Han Empire.

to the north in 129 B.C. Other expeditions followed Zhang Qian's return, conquering more land for China to the north and west. Zhang Qian himself went on a second journey westward in 115 B.C., during which he gathered more information about civilizations such as Bactria, Fergana, and Parthia. (See map.) This information encouraged Wudi to send another army westward in 104 B.C. and, after three years, it managed to defeat Fergana and add large parts of Central Asia to the empire. Under Wudi, the Han Empire also took control of southern Manchuria and the southeast coast of China, as well as conquering the peoples of the Mekong Valley and much of northern Korea.

TRADE IN THE HAN DYNASTY

For many years, the Chinese were the only people in the world who knew how to spin silk thread and weave it into cloth. (See pages 51–52.) This made silk into a very valuable commodity. It was probably already being traded beyond China's borders at the time of the First Emperor. During the Han dynasty, this trade expanded greatly, and Chinese silk was sold

A CLOSER LOOK

Probably very few traders made the complete journey along the Silk Road from Ch'ang-an to Antioch. Instead, each merchant did part of the journey, carrying his goods on a camel caravan from one trading center to the next. There he would sell or exchange his goods with another merchant before returning to the city he had set out from. The second merchant would then take the goods another stage along the road, and the process would be repeated.

A pottery model of a silk merchant from the 6th century A.D.

in markets throughout Asia, Arabia, East Africa, around the Mediterranean Sea, and throughout the Roman Empire. Some of the silk was transported by sea, using a route to India, then into either the Persian Gulf or the Red Sea. Pottery, ceramics, and spices also traveled by this sea route. However, most silk went by land, along a route known as the Silk Road. The Silk Road stretched from Ch'ang-an in northern China to Antioch in what is now Turkey. It had many branches along the way to connect it to other important cities and trading centers. In exchange for their silk, the traders brought back jewels from India, jade from Central Asia, and gold, spices, and glassware from the Middle East and the Mediterranean. There was a good market for those in China.

A CLOSER LOOK

The Silk Road was an unpaved track, which wound its way through mountains and deserts. Traveling along it was never easy since the deserts were hot and dusty in summer, and the mountain passes were blocked by snow in winter. There was also the constant danger of attack by wild animals or robbers. To make the journey more comfortable, a series of caravansaries developed along the way. These were small, walled towns where traders and their animals could rest in safety and obtain fresh supplies.

To ensure that the emperor received his share of the profits, customs posts were set up along the Chinese borders to collect heavy taxes on all goods being moved in or out of the country. Wudi also added to the emperor's income by taking control of the production of both iron and salt in China, and keeping all the profits for himself.

THE LATER HAN

Toward the end of the first century B.C., the Han dynasty was led by a series of weaker emperors. The prosperity of the empire declined, the peasant farmers struggled to pay their taxes and many fell into debt. Bad harvests and disease brought many deaths. Some peasants became bandits, living in the hills and joining secret societies such as the Red Eyebrows and the Green Woodsmen. These societies led the peasants in revolt and in A.D. 9 a new leader, Wang Mang, took control of the country. His rule

The Chinese obtained most of their salt from the ground in the form of brine or salty water. They extracted the brine by digging wells into which they lowered a hollow bamboo pipe on a rope. When the pipe was filled, it was raised to the surface by a windlass turned by oxen. The brine was then heated until the water evaporated, leaving the salt crystals behind.

lasted until A.D. 25 when the Han took over once again. This second period of Han rule is known as the Later Han, and the first period is often referred to as the Former Han.

Much of Ch'ang-an had been destroyed in the fighting, so a new capital was built in Luoyang. As China flourished again, the population started to increase. By the start of the 3rd century there was not enough land for all the peasants to have farms. Many had no means of making money to buy food or pay their taxes. In A.D. 184 rebellions broke out once more, this time led by a secret society known as the Yellow Turbans. The rebels were finally defeated in 204, but the government was still weak and corrupt. Wealthy families began to gain political power and nomads from the north began to attack China again. Then the leaders of the army rebelled against their rulers and, in A.D. 220, the last of the Han emperors gave up his throne.

A CLOSER LOOK

Some of the most spectacular archaeological discoveries of recent times have come from the tombs of the wealthy from the Han dynasty. People believed that there would be a life after death that would be like the one they had already lived, and so they were buried with all the objects they might need. These included silk clothes and other artifacts, as well as food and drink. There were also models of farmhouses, boats, and carts to represent what the dead person had owned in life. Other models represented servants, who would look after the dead person in the next life, and also musicians, dancers, jugglers, and acrobats.

These pottery figures of entertainers come from a Han dynasty tomb.

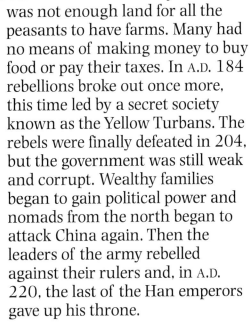

THE ARRIVAL OF BUDDHISM

During Later Han times, the faith known as Buddhism arrived in China. This religion started in India in the 6th century B.C., and knowledge of it spread along the Silk Road to China by about A.D. 100. Buddhism taught that people should lead a good and simple life, so it fitted well with the ideas of Confucianism and Daoism. Many Chinese people began to base their lives and their outlook on all three beliefs.

CHAOS AND DIVISION

After the fall of the Han dynasty the empire split into three kingdoms, Wei in the north, Shu in the west, and Wu in the south and east. The nomads invaded from the north, and in A.D. 383 they reached the Yangtze River. The Chinese managed to defeat them and prevent them from invading southern China, but the country was divided once more, with the Yangtze River marking the boundary between the north and the south. Then, in 581, Emperor Wendi took the throne of the Northern kingdom and founded the Sui dynasty.

A CLOSER LOOK

During the troubled times after the fall of the Han dynasty, many Chinese people turned to Buddhism as a way of helping them cope with their problems. Some even made pilgrimages to India. The most famous of these pilgrims was Faxian, who set out from central China in A.D. 399. His journey took him over the Himalayas and through northwest India until he reached the mouth of the Ganges River. There he stayed for many years, before finally arriving back in China in 414. He kept a detailed account of his experiences, which were later published in a book called *Records of Buddhist Kingdoms*.

A Buddhist monk in present-day China.

THE SUI DYNASTY

Emperor Wendi set out to reunite China. He sent
an army across the Yangtze River to reconquer the
Southern kingdom. He encouraged agriculture by
setting up better irrigation projects that carried
water from the rivers to the fields and made it possible
to grow more rice and other grain crops. All of these
measures helped to restore wealth to the country
and allowed Wendi to reduce the amount of taxes
people had to pay. Wendi also cut the amount of
time that people had to spend in the army.

These moves made Wendi popular, but his son
and successor, Yangdi, undid all his father's good
work when he came to power in 604. Yangdi started
by ordering everyone to pay ten years' taxes in
advance. This was to pay for the building of palaces
and pleasure parks for himself, as well as for repairs
to the Great Wall and for work on the Grand Canal.
The Grand Canal had been started in the Zhou
dynasty as a series of small canals linking the Yangtze
and Yellow Rivers. This system remained in use until

*Traffic on the present-
day Grand Canal.
Between 1958 and
1964, the canal was
straightened, widened,
and dredged to make it
possible for barges of
up to 600 tons to
travel along its
whole length.*

Emperor Yangdi celebrated the opening of the Grand Canal by going on a cruise with his family, his officials, and members of his court. His boat was at the head of a procession that is said to have stretched for 62 miles (100 km) along the canal. It is said that 80,000 laborers were needed to tow the boats.

Emperor Yangdi's boat on the Grand Canal.

the Sui dynasty, but Yangdi decided to improve on it. His new canal partly followed the line of one of the old canals, but was much wider and deeper. Starting near Hangzhou, it connected the Yangtze and the Yellow Rivers at Luoyang and eventually extended from there to Beijing, a distance of more than 684 miles (1,100 km). It was used mainly to transport armies to the northern regions of the country, in barges towed by forced labor. But it was also an important route for carrying cargoes of rice from the south to the north, as well as other goods and people.

THE END OF THE SUI DYNASTY

In addition to taking money from people in taxes, Yangdi forced thousands of peasants to leave their farms and work on his building projects, often in terrible conditions. He also conscripted many more people to join his army when he set out to try and reconquer Korea. This campaign was unsuccessful. In 617 the people started to rebel against him. The army also rose up against him and, in 618, Yangdi was assassinated. Another dynasty had come to an end.

THE TANG DYNASTY

After Yangdi's death, Li Yuan became the first ruler of the Tang dynasty. He made Ch'ang-an into the capital once more and set about reuniting the country. Under his son, Taizong, who reigned from 626–649, China started to extend its influence beyond its boundaries in the west to bring the great trade routes of central Asia under its control. At the same time, trade by sea increased, and ports along the Chinese coast became bustling centers of commerce. The increase in trade brought great prosperity to the country and also brought direct contact with large numbers of foreigners, for the first time in Chinese history. Industry, arts, and crafts flourished. The Buddhist religion became increasingly important, and by the 8th century there were over 300,000 Buddhist monks in China, as well as many shrines and temples to the Buddhist faith.

The peace and stability of the early Tang dynasty ensured that this period was one of the most glorious and prosperous in Chinese history. But it did not last forever. The last great Tang ruler was Xuanzong, who reigned from 712 to 756. When he was nearly 60, he fell in love with one of his concubines, Yang Guifei, showering her with gifts. Xuanzong also confided in another courtier, An Lushan, who was a favorite of Yang Guifei. But

This painting from the Tang dynasty shows Xuanzong and Yang Guifei trying to escape from An Lushan at the time of his rebellion in 755.

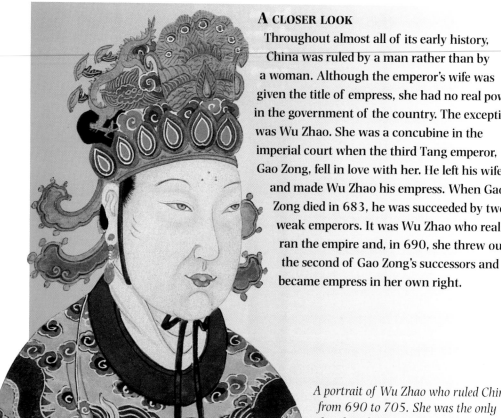

*A portrait of Wu Zhao who ruled China
from 690 to 705. She was the only
female to become a "Son of Heaven."*

An Lushan was cunning and used his power and
influence to gather an army of 160,000 men.
In 755 An Lushan led a revolt against Xuanzong
and forced the emperor to have Yang Guifei strangled.
In the following year, Xuanzong abdicated in favor
of his son.

The Tang dynasty continued, but it was much
weakened. Wealth began to decline, and China
became less important internationally. This led to
opposition to foreign influences in China, including
the Buddhist faith. During the 840s, Buddhist
monks and nuns were forced to return to ordinary
lives, and their monasteries, temples, and shrines
were destroyed or closed down. By 900 the Tang
empire had almost collapsed, and in 907 the people
rebelled again. The last Tang emperor was defeated,
and China split up once more, this time into five
separate kingdoms.

THE SONG DYNASTY

In the following 53 years, five emperors tried to reunite China, but none of them succeeded. Then in 960 an army general, called Zhao Kuang Yin, was proclaimed emperor by his soldiers. He became the first emperor of the Song dynasty. By 979 he had reunited the country once more.

During the 11th and 12th centuries China was probably the wealthiest country in the world. Many farming families added to their income by making wine, paper, charcoal, and textiles, and growing crops such as tea, bamboo, and sugarcane. There were large workshops in the towns and cities making silk, lacquerware, pottery, porcelain, and paper for books and documents. Iron-making and shipbuilding also increased as trade continued to grow.

This detail is taken from a scroll depicting life in 12th-century China. It shows a busy scene, possibly in the Song capital, Kaifeng.

Problems began in 1126, however, when a northern tribe called the Jin attacked China. The Jin overran about one-third of the country, including the capital, Kaifeng. The emperor and most of his family were taken prisoner and never seen again, but one son escaped. He set up a new capital in Hangzhou and became the first emperor of the Southern Song dynasty. But, in less than 100 years, the lands ruled by the Jin and the Southern Song were threatened by other invaders from the north—the Mongols. (See 57–59.)

CHINESE SOCIETY

The emperor was the most important person in Imperial China. Beneath him, society was split into four main groups. They were known as the Shi, the Nong, the Gong, and the Shang.

THE SHI

Beneath the emperor, the Shi was the most important group in Chinese society. It was made up mainly of nobles and scholars, including poets and philosophers. The nobles prided themselves on not having to do any hard, physical work. They spent a lot of their

A scene at the court of the Tang emperors. The beautifully dressed wives and daughters of noblemen enjoy a feast while being entertained by musicians.

time at court and often had a house in the capital city of that time. These town houses were like small palaces themselves, standing three or four stories high. Outside, the houses were brightly painted, while inside they were decorated with painted screens and silk hangings, as well as many beautiful ornaments. Noble families also had large country estates that they visited. These provided their income through rents and produce.

THE NONG

The Nong was the largest group in Chinese society and was made up of peasant farmers and their families. Although many peasants were poor and uneducated, they were considered important because they worked hard and provided food for the empire. Even on small farms there was usually enough work to keep the family busy every day. Farmers had to grow enough grain to pay their taxes, feed themselves until the next harvest, and

A CLOSER LOOK

During the 10th century A.D., a new fashion started for noblewomen to have tiny feet. This was partly because small feet were seen to be more beautiful than normal-sized feet. It was also a way of restricting noblewomen's freedom. To ensure that a female baby's feet stayed small, they were doubled over shortly after birth and then bandaged tightly. This broke the bones in the arch of the foot and turned the toes underneath. The foot grew to only about half the normal length. This method of foot-binding was terribly painful and meant that many women could barely walk.

These costly shoes were made for bound feet.

A 20th-century farmer near Quanzhou plows his land with an ox-drawn plow, just as his ancestors would have done.

have seeds left over to plant for the next crop. From the middle of the Han dynasty, well-off farmers used oxen to pull plows with iron-tipped blades that cut deep furrows into their fields, but the poorer farmers had to rely on wooden plows that they pushed themselves.

The Nong often suffered badly in times of war or rebellion. At any time after the age of 15, peasant men could be drafted into the army or forced to work on one of the emperor's building projects. Conditions were harsh, and many men died of overwork, cold, hunger, or disease.

THE GONG

The third group in Chinese society, the Gong, was made up of the many different craftworkers. They produced beautiful and practical objects from gold, brass, bronze, iron, and jade, as well as making pottery, porcelain, and lacquerware. Others were carpenters and builders, makers of ornamental roof-tiles, or of carts and wagons. Most craftworkers lived in the large towns and cities since this was where there was a market for their goods.

THE SHANG

The least-respected group in Chinese society was the Shang. This group was made up of merchants and traders. Many merchants were very rich, but even the wealthiest were thought to be less important than the poorest farmer. This was because merchants and traders produced nothing themselves. Instead, they made their living from the work of others. Everyone despised them because of this, and many restrictions were placed upon them. For example, they were not allowed to wear silk robes or to ride on horseback or carry weapons. However, it eventually became possible for the sons of merchants and traders to leave the Shang class by taking examinations to become government officials or civil servants.

Children were taught to obey their parents throughout their lives. Even when they were adults themselves, they were expected to bow when they met their parents formally.

THE IMPORTANCE OF THE FAMILY

In all social groups, the family played a very important role in Chinese life. Confucius taught that children should obey their parents throughout their lives—even when they were adults with children of their own. The oldest man in the family had control over all its belongings. He also had the right to approve or disapprove of the marriages arranged for his children and his grandchildren by the women of the family. When a girl was married she had to move to her husband's home. There she was expected to obey her mother-in-law as well as her husband, and was only treated really well if she gave birth to several sons.

Every year the Chinese held a special spring festival, called Qing Ming, at which they offered sacrifices to their ancestors. These sacrifices were usually gifts of food. After the food had been offered, the people usually had a special feast in which they ate the food themselves.

Today many Chinese people honor their ancestors at the Qing Ming festival by burning incense and offering them gifts.

ANCESTORS

Besides respecting the living, the Chinese had great respect for their ancestors. In the Zhou dynasty (see page 10) special temples were built where ancestors were remembered. In later times, Chinese families wrote their ancestors' names on a special wooden board that they kept in their homes. Because they believed in a life after death, even the poorest Chinese buried their dead with as many items as they could afford, to accompany the dead person to the next life. They also looked on their ancestors as part of the living family, asking their advice on family problems and telling them about important family events, such as the birth of a baby or a wedding.

RUNNING THE COUNTRY

In addition to close advisers who lived at court with him, each emperor had many thousands of officials to help him run the country. Some of these officials were scholars, poets, and artists. Others were engineers who were employed to build bridges, canals, and irrigation projects. Many were needed to collect the taxes that helped to pay for the huge building projects that most emperors undertook. Sometimes these taxes were collected as money, but more often they were collected as a proportion of the farmer's grain harvest.

To become government officials, young men had to spend many years studying. They also had to take difficult examinations. Those who passed the district examination went on to study for three more years. Then, they took the provincial examination in which they had to write essays on government and on Confucius's works and ideas. After this came the palace examination. Students had to stay in the examination room from sunrise to sunset for this exam. They wrote just one long essay on a subject chosen by the examiners.

A bronze model of a high-ranking government official from the Han dynasty. His chariot and horse were provided by the government.

LAWS AND PUNISHMENTS

The emperor had the power of life and death over everyone in his empire. His laws had to be obeyed without question and, if they were not, people were often severely punished. In the reign of Qin Shi Huangdi, who was influenced by the harsh Legalist ideas of his adviser Li Si (see page 15), these punishments are said to have included beheading, being torn apart by chariots, or being cut in two. If someone was found outside their village without a permit, their nose and ears could be cut off. However, from the Han dynasty onward, emperors were influenced by Confucianism, and their laws were less severe than those of Qin Shi Huangdi. The main punishment for wrongdoers was work for long periods on projects such as building canals, palaces, and tombs.

EVERYDAY LIFE

Everyday life for the Chinese people varied according to whether they lived in the town or the countryside, and whether they were rich or poor. But whoever they were and wherever they lived, people needed three basic things in order to survive: food, clothes, and shelter.

FOOD AND COOKING

Once they settled down and started farming (see page 9), the Chinese realized that their land was more suited to growing crops than to raising large herds of cattle. As a result, grains, vegetables, and fruit became the most important part of the Chinese diet. Very little dairy produce was eaten. At the time of Qin Shi Huangdi, people in the north grew millet and wheat as their main grains, but in the south and east of the country people grew rice. During the

Rice-growing methods have not changed much in 2,000 years. This man is carrying rice plants to the fields to be planted. The fields are kept wet until the rice has grown and ripened. Then they are drained, and the crop is harvested.

A CLOSER LOOK

Some fishermen used cormorants to help them catch fish. The birds dived off the boat and caught the fish in their beaks. A ring around their throats stopped them from swallowing the fish, while a long rope around one of their legs prevented them from flying away.

Today, some fishermen still use cormorants to catch fish for them.

Song dynasty, better irrigation systems together with new varieties of rice allowed the rice farmers to harvest two crops a year. Rice quickly became the most common grain throughout China. Besides being boiled, steamed, or fried, it was also ground to make flour, and fermented to make wine.

One popular way of preparing food was to cut it into small pieces and cook it quickly in an iron frying-pan, called a wok, on the top of a stove. People also enjoyed stews and food that had been cooked by steaming in a double saucepan. To add flavor, many different herbs and spices were used. They included ginger, garlic, sesame seeds, aniseed, and chili peppers. Once food was cooked, it was served in pottery bowls and eaten with chopsticks.

Much of our knowledge of food in Imperial China comes from the remains of food left in tombs. These food remains have dried out over the centuries, but most of them can still be recognized today. The richest tombs sometimes contained lists of food items, together with recipes, and hints for cooking them.

A CLOSER LOOK

Chinese farmers grew vegetables, such as leeks, onions, Chinese cabbage, lentils, lotus shoots, soybeans, mung beans, and bamboo shoots, and fruit crops, such as apricots, peaches, melons, strawberries, pears, plums, and persimmons. Meat for poorer people included chicken, duck, goose, pork, and dog, but rich people also ate meat from deer, tigers, bears, sparrows, owls, hares, doves, and pheasants. Both rich and poor ate fish.

39

CLOTHES

We have learned a lot about the clothes worn in Imperial China from paintings, pottery, and from actual clothes found in the tombs of wealthy people. From this evidence we know that basic fashions did not change much over the centuries. Rich men and women both wore long robes that were made from silk and fastened at the waist with a belt or sash. For summer, the silk was fine and gauze-like, but winter robes were made from heavy silk, such as brocade or satin. Under their robes, the women sometimes wore trousers that were tight at the ankles. Men and women also wore silk stockings and slippers, and shoes or boots made from silk or fine leather. In the coldest weather, they also wore furs and embroidered vests over their robes.

The color and pattern of silk were often used to show a person's position in society. For example, only the emperor was allowed to wear a yellow robe decorated with a five-clawed dragon, while the most important government officials could wear robes with a crane on it.

Two princesses from the Tang dynasty. Their long sleeves, turned-up shoes, and elaborate hairstyles were the height of fashion and only suited to a life of leisure.

The most important army officials could wear robes decorated with a unicorn.

Farmers and craftworkers needed clothes that were cheap and practical, but again both men and women dressed in a similar style. They wore a short tunic fastened at the waist with a belt, and a pair of trousers that ended just below the knee. They probably also wore stockings and sandals made from marsh plants or straw. The material for these clothes was made from yarn spun from plant fibers. The most common was hemp, which was grown on farms in the north and west of the country, but grasses and coarse, often prickly herbs were also used. Clothes for the summer were made from one layer of material, but

those for the winter were made
from several layers sewn together.
On days when it was really cold,
farmers and their families wore
sheepskins around their shoulders
to keep themselves warm.

HOUSES

Both in towns and in the
countryside, the homes of the
wealthy were large and had many
rooms. These houses were usually built around at
least two courtyards and were surrounded by a high
wall with a gate, which was sometimes protected
with a gatehouse.

The houses of the poor were much smaller. They
often had only one room in which the whole family
cooked, ate, and slept. Until the time of the Tang
dynasty, when chairs were first introduced, neither
the rich nor the poor had much furniture. The rich
probably had beds with feather pillows, but poor
people slept on rush mats on the floor and lay their
heads on pillows made from pottery or wood.
If they wanted to sit down, people used
mats or lounged on wooden couches.
Chinese towns were built in a square
or oblong shape and surrounded by
walls made of hard-packed soil.
Inside, more walls divided
a town into wards or
districts, separating
the rich from the
poor. During the
day people could
go from one ward to
another, but at night
the gates to each ward
were locked. The streets
were not paved, so they
were dry and dusty in
the summer and muddy
during the winter.

*In the Han dynasty,
pottery models of
houses were often
buried in tombs.*

ENTERTAINING THE PEOPLE

Rich people had the most leisure time and therefore the greatest choice of entertainment. Noblemen went hunting on horseback, taking dogs with them and shooting their prey with bows and arrows. They also played polo and a kind of soccer. Noblewomen and their daughters spent time talking and drinking tea, listening to music (see page 32), and playing games with cards, dice, and counters, as well as playing a form of charades. In their homes, or in the imperial palace, the wealthy were entertained by troupes of acrobats, jugglers, singers, and dancers. Some of these troupes also performed in the open air where they were watched by the ordinary people. Games of chance were popular with everyone, and people gambled their money.

GETTING AROUND

The Chinese had many different vehicles for transporting people and goods. The simplest was the wheelbarrow, which was first designed for moving people and later used for moving goods. Oxcarts were used for carrying people as well as goods. They traveled slowly but could carry very heavy loads. The most important government officials traveled in fast-moving carts or chariots, pulled by horses and driven by servants (see page 37). Less important officials traveled in carts pulled by oxen. The invention of the horse collar made it possible for horses to pull heavy loads (see page 44), while the introduction of stirrups made horseback riding safer. However, traders who used the Silk Road carried their goods on the backs of camels, since these animals were better suited to the dry desert conditions.

In Tang times, polo became a popular sport for both men and women at court. It was very similar to the game that is played today.

TRADE WITHIN CHINA

Each town in China had at least one market, and large cities such as Ch'ang-an had several. The local farmers came to these markets to sell their surplus produce. This might be fruit or vegetables, or livestock, such as chickens, ducks, geese, or pigs. Even if the animals were being sold for food, they were brought to the market alive and killed only after they had been sold. Other stalls sold everyday items such as baskets, pots, pans, salt, rice, and firewood. Craftworkers had stalls, too, selling items made from jade, ivory, bronze, brass, and lacquerware. Cloth made from silk was on sale for those who could afford it, and cloth made from hemp was available for everyone else.

This busy street scene is possibly in the Song capital, Kaifeng. Among other things, it shows goods being unloaded from a cart, and a camel caravan setting off to transport other goods to distant parts of the world.

SCIENCE AND TECHNOLOGY

The Chinese were practical people. Many of their inventions and discoveries came about as a result of trying to solve everyday problems. Because of this, we do not always know who invented certain objects or even when they were invented. These inventions include the compass, paper, the wheelbarrow, the odometer, which was used for measuring the distance traveled by wheeled vehicles, and the horse collar that rested on a horse's chest muscles rather than on its neck, allowing it to pull a heavy load without choking. Neither do we know who was responsible for many of the discoveries in science and medicine, but it seems likely that, like the inventions, they were based on the ideas of more than one person.

Acupuncture is still used throughout the world to treat many different illnesses and health problems.

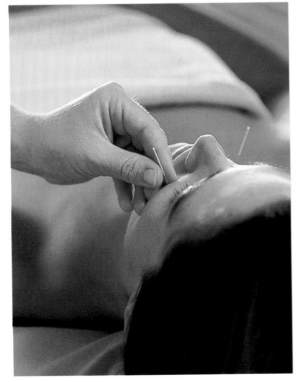

MEDICINE

The people of Imperial China believed that illnesses were caused by the opposing forces of *yin* and *yang* (see page 13) becoming unbalanced in the body. They thought that this balance could be restored by using a mixture of herbal remedies, a good diet, and acupuncture. Some herbs were made into medicines, pills, and ointments. Others were added to soups that were eaten by the whole family.

Acupuncture is based on the belief that there is a life force that flows along 12 lines, or meridians, in the body. Each of these meridians is linked to

A CLOSER LOOK

Lady Xin, Marchioness of Dai, died in about 168 BC. Yet the body was in very good condition when her tomb was excavated in 1972. Medical experts examined the body and found evidence that Lady Xin had suffered from tuberculosis and gallstones. She was in her 50s when she died, and her spine was deformed with age. She had parasites in her intestines and a fracture to her right arm that had been badly set. She also suffered from heart disease, for which she had been prescribed a mixture of cinnamon, peppercorns, and magnolia bark.

a different organ. If very fine needles are inserted into various points along these meridians, they can relieve pain and help to cure illnesses. The Chinese have used acupuncture for over 2,000 years. Scientists today believe that acupuncture works by encouraging the brain to release endorphins, which are the body's natural painkillers.

ALCHEMY AND THE ELIXIR OF LIFE

Alchemists used a mixture of science and magic (alchemy) to try and perform three impossible tasks: to change metals such as lead into gold, to make a medicine that would cure all ills, and to make a potion that would make people live forever. This potion was known as the Elixir of Life. The Chinese alchemists spent much of their time trying to discover how to make it. All their attempts failed — and some of their potions were more likely to kill people, since they contained poisonous substances, such as mercury!

However, during the course of their experiments, alchemists often made unexpected and useful discoveries. One such discovery happened in the 8th century, when a Chinese alchemist accidentally learned how to make gunpowder when he tried to mix a potion that included charcoal, saltpeter, and sulfur. The mixture is said to have exploded and set his beard on fire! At first, gunpowder was used in fireworks and to make loud explosions to frighten an enemy in battle. But by the 10th

Knowledge of gunpowder was brought to the West by Arab traders and is still used in spectacular fireworks.

A CLOSER LOOK

In A.D. 132 a court astronomer named Zhang Heng made a device for detecting earthquakes. It consisted of a bronze vase with eight dragons' heads fastened to it. Each dragon had a ball in its mouth and pointed in a different direction. Opposite each dragon was a bronze toad with its mouth open. When there was an earthquake the vase shook, making the dragon facing the center of the earthquake spit its ball into the mouth of the nearest toad. Although this early seismograph could not predict earthquakes, at least it showed which direction they were coming from.

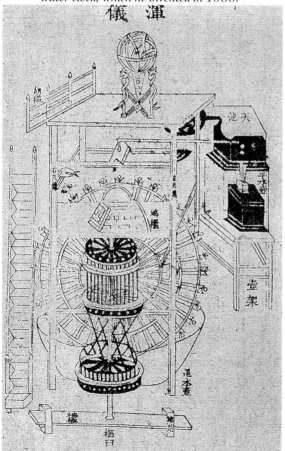

This diagram shows the workings of Su Song's water clock, which he invented in 1088.

century, it was also being used in weapons. The earliest of these weapons were fire arrows. A fire arrow had a small amount of gunpowder wrapped around its head. A fuse was attached and lit before the arrow was fired. Later, fuses were attached to balls of gunpowder, and these were shot at the enemy from a catapult.

ASTRONOMY, TIME, AND NAVIGATION

The Chinese were skilled astronomers. As early as the 2nd century B.C., there was an imperial observatory from which scientists watched the movements of the stars and planets in the night sky. They also studied the sun and the moon and calculated that there were 365.25 days in a year. Toward the end of the 11th century A.D., a government official called Su Song invented a clock that not only told the time of day but also tracked the orbits (paths) of stars and planets. It was driven by a waterwheel inside a tower and made it possible for an accurate calendar to be drawn up.

Some time before 200 B.C. the Chinese discovered the amazing properties of magnetic rock, or lodestone. When a lodestone is floated in a dish of water, or allowed to swing freely on a thread, it will always swing around to point in a north-south direction. At first, the Chinese used lodestones in town planning, to make sure that the town and its houses were facing in a direction that was in harmony with nature. Later, lodestones were used as simple compasses for finding directions on land. By the 1180s the Chinese had developed, a maritime compass, which helped them to travel long distances by sea.

PAPER AND PRINTING

At the time of the First Emperor, documents were written on strips of bamboo, fastened together with leather thongs. During the Han dynasty, people began to look for something that was lighter, as well as longer-lasting. In about A.D. 59, it was discovered that a smooth sheet could be made from mashed up silkworm cocoons (see page 51). This paper sheet was ideal for writing on, but very expensive to produce. So people began to experiment with different materials in the hope of finding a cheaper method of making paper. Around A.D. 105, a government official called Cai Lun began to encourage the papermakers to experiment with bark, chopped up rags, old fishing nets, and the roots of hemp and other plants. Eventually a suitable mixture was found.

Cheap paper led to more books being written, although they all had to be copied by hand. Then, in the 9th century, wood-block printing began to develop on a large scale. To make books in this way, all the text and illustrations for a single page were cut in reverse onto a block of wood so that the parts to be printed stood up above the rest of the surface. The block was inked and then pressed onto a sheet

Bound books like this one being held did not become popular in China until the Tang dynasty. Before that, most books were produced as scrolls, rolls of paper.

A CLOSER LOOK

Rather than putting their coins in purses to carry them around, the Chinese used the hole in the middle of the coins to thread them onto a string. These strings were heavy to carry, and so merchants got into the habit of leaving them in the care of someone they could trust. In exchange, this person would give the merchant a piece of paper with the amount written on it. The idea of paper money gradually developed from this and was in common use by the Song dynasty.

The Diamond Sutra *is a sacred Buddhist scroll which was printed in 868. It is the oldest-known printed text in the world and the first to have a date printed on it.*

of paper to make one page of a book. The block could be used many times, but a new one had to be carved for each page. In the Song dynasty, a printer called Bi Sheng invented movable type. This meant that the same type could be used and reset for different pages. But, since the Chinese language has at least 80,000 separate symbols, it was a long time before movable type completely replaced wood-block printing.

IRRIGATION AND CIVIL ENGINEERING

Water was always a problem in Imperial China. Sometimes there was too much, and the land was flooded, but at other times there was not enough, and the crops died in the fields from lack of moisture. To try and solve these problems, the emperors employed engineers to build dams and islands in some rivers to control their flow. Small canals and drainage ditches were dug to carry water to the fields in times of drought, and to allow it to

In the 12th century, foot-powered pumps were used to raise water from irrigation ditches to flood the rice fields.

run back to the river in times of flooding. Because the fields were usually higher than the river, pumps and waterwheels were used to lift the water from one level to another.

Other engineers were employed to design and build bridges across rivers and steep ravines. Bridges of wood or stone were built across rivers that flowed between low banks. However, bridges suspended from strong bamboo poles were used where the river banks were steep and the river itself was narrow. By the Sui dynasty, the Chinese had discovered how to make strong chains from wrought iron. These could be used to make suspension bridges up to 330 feet (100 m) long.

A CLOSER LOOK

Iron working came under government control in 119 B.C. At that time there were about 50 iron foundries, each with large blast furnaces built from heat-resistant bricks. Iron was cheaper to produce than bronze, so it was used for tools and weapons. Some of the tools were iron plowshares that could cut more deeply into the soil than the old, wooden ones. The introduction of iron tools allowed farmers to work more efficiently and grow more crops on their land.

ARTS AND CRAFTS

This pottery figure was discovered in a Tang dynasty tomb. The coloring comes from the glaze.

The people of Imperial China were skilled artists and craftworkers. They produced many beautiful things from pottery, silk, bronze, brass, gold, silver, jade, and ivory, as well as painting pictures, writing poetry, and making music to which they could sing and dance.

POTTERY AND PORCELAIN

The Chinese first made pottery around 8,000 years ago. Their early methods of shaping pots included smearing clay inside baskets or wooden bowls, molding a ball of clay in the hands, and coiling long strips of clay on top of each other. Between 3000 and 2400 B.C., they learned how to shape their pots on a potter's wheel. These early pots had a dull finish and a very rough surface. Some time during the Bronze Age, the Chinese discovered how to make a glaze. This was a liquid that was painted onto the pots before they were baked and which gave them a smooth, shiny surface. Glazes were usually colorless, but sometimes different minerals were added that created streaks of color as they melted in the heat.

At first, pottery was used for practical items such as storage jars, jugs, and bowls, but later it was also used for decorative objects such as vases and for figures of people, animals, and houses. From the Han dynasty on, large numbers of these pottery figures were buried with the wealthy when they died. They represented the real servants, musicians, and other entertainers who in the Shang and Zhou dynasties would have been killed and buried with the dead person.

A CLOSER LOOK

Figures found in tombs include acrobats, jugglers, dancers, and musicians. There are also people riding horses, playing board games, traveling on camels and in oxcarts, preparing food, cooking, and doing household chores, such as washing. Most of these figures are only an inch or so high.

Many of these figures have now been excavated, adding to our knowledge of life in Imperial China by showing such details as the clothes people wore and the activities in which they were involved.

During the Tang dynasty, the Chinese discovered how to make a type of porcelain. Porcelain was much finer than pottery. It was very hard and shiny and made a ringing noise when it was tapped with a fingernail. It was made from a fine white clay, called kaolin or china clay, mixed with water and a powdered stone called petuntse. When the porcelain was baked in a kiln, or large oven, at temperatures of 2,642° F (1,450° C), the petuntse melted to make a glassy surface. Like pottery, porcelain was also used for bowls, jars, vases, and figures.

Long strands of silk hanging in the Silk Market in Shanghai. Silk is still an important product in China today.

PRODUCING SILK

No one is certain exactly when the Chinese first discovered how to make silk cloth, but the earliest known piece can be dated back to around 2700 B.C. However, there is evidence that people knew about silk long before this date, as in the northeast of China some small stone ornaments that look like silkworms have been found. These ornaments date back to around 4000 B.C.

The fiber used to make silk cloth comes from the cocoon around the caterpillar of the silkworm moth. Each cocoon has a fiber, up to 2,950 feet (900 m) long. To remove the fiber from the cocoon, the cocoon is dropped into boiling water. This melts the sticky secretion that holds the cocoon together. Then the fiber is unraveled and cleaned. Each silk fiber is so fine that several have to be twisted together to make a thread strong enough to weave into cloth. This means that many thousands of cocoons are needed for every yard (m) of cloth.

51

It was difficult to gather thousands of silkworm cocoons from the wild, so the Chinese began to raise silkworms in special buildings. In these buildings, the amount of heat, light, and air were all controlled to try and get all the moths to mate and lay their eggs at the same time. When the eggs hatched, the silkworms were put on bamboo trays and fed on mulberry leaves until they started spinning their cocoons. Some cocoons were allowed to turn into moths so that the breeding process could start again, but the rest were dropped into boiling water to unwind their silk fiber.

This 17th-century picture shows women processing silkworm cocoons, in order to turn the silk fiber into a thread strong enough to be woven into cloth.

MAKING CLOTH

Silk thread was woven into cloth by hand using a horizontal loom. By using different thicknesses of thread, the weavers produced different thicknesses of cloth. Patterns were woven in by raising different threads as the cloth was being woven, or by using different colored threads for the warp (lengthwise threads) and the weft (crosswise threads).

A CLOSER LOOK

Legend says that the secret of making silk was discovered accidentally by Xi Ling Shi, the wife of a mythical king, Huangdi. Huangdi noticed that something was eating the leaves on his mulberry trees and asked his gardeners to find out what it was. They discovered that little caterpillars were causing the damage. They also discovered some cocoons nearby. These cocoons fascinated Xi Ling Shi so much that she took them inside to look at them more closely. While she was studying them, one fell into a bowl of hot water and, to her surprise, a fine thread began to unwind from it.

LACQUERWARE

Long before the time of the First Emperor, the Chinese had discovered how to decorate wooden objects with a liquid called lacquer. Lacquer was made from the sap of the lacquer tree and started out as a gray, sticky

A lacquerware cup from the Song dynasty. Many lacquerware items have been excavated from tombs. These look as good as when they were first buried, up to 2,000 years ago.

substance. As it was heated and mixed with oil, it turned into a thin liquid that could be painted on ornaments, trays, bowls, and boxes. When dry, the lacquer was a brown-black color which became very hard and could be polished until it shone like glass. Red was often added to make a colored lacquer. Gold and silver were also used.

METALWORK

The Chinese were skilled at using various metals for both practical and decorative purposes. During the Shang dynasty, bronze was used for tools and weapons, and for huge ceremonial vessels in which food and wine were offered as sacrifices (see pages 9 and 54). By the time of the First Emperor, iron had largely replaced bronze for tools and weapons, but bronze was still used for many decorative objects. It was often intricately

A CLOSER LOOK

In the Qin dynasty, the Chinese must have known how to treat iron to make it extremely hard and prevent it from rusting. We know this because some of the swords in Qin Shi Huangdi's tomb are still shiny and sharp enough to split a human hair.

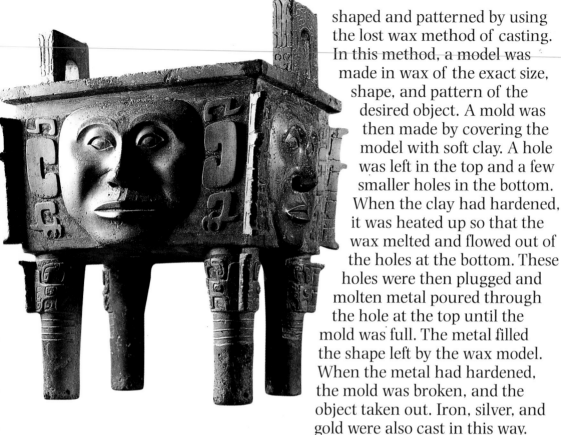

shaped and patterned by using the lost wax method of casting. In this method, a model was made in wax of the exact size, shape, and pattern of the desired object. A mold was then made by covering the model with soft clay. A hole was left in the top and a few smaller holes in the bottom. When the clay had hardened, it was heated up so that the wax melted and flowed out of the holes at the bottom. These holes were then plugged and molten metal poured through the hole at the top until the mold was full. The metal filled the shape left by the wax model. When the metal had hardened, the mold was broken, and the object taken out. Iron, silver, and gold were also cast in this way.

This large bronze vessel is from the Shang dynasty and was probably used to hold food at important ceremonies.

CARVING JADE

Long before they discovered how to use metals, the Chinese used a hard stone called jade to make tools and weapons, such as knives and axheads. Early peoples carved jade into disks, known as *bi*, and columns, known as *cong*, but we have no evidence to tell us what these jade carvings represented. They also made jade into tiny figures and ornaments, by rubbing the stone with abrasive sand to get the

A jade burial suit from the late 2nd century B.C. It is made up of around 2,000 wafer-thin tablets of jade, held together with gold wire.

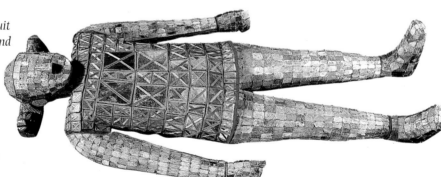

Mirrors made from bronze were very popular. They were usually heavily patterned on the reverse and highly polished on the front to show a clear reflection. Qin Shi Huangdi is said to have had one that was 7 feet (2 m) across. In addition to showing the reflection of anyone standing in front of it, it was said to reveal their internal organs and their innermost thoughts!

The reverse side of a bronze mirror from the Tang dynasty. It is patterned with flowers, four monkeys, and a toad.

shape they wanted. This ornamental use continued throughout imperial times, when jade disks were hung together to make a form of wind chime. Known to the Chinese as *yü*, jade was associated with purity and nobleness. During the Han dynasty some wealthy people were even buried in jade suits, since it was believed that jade would preserve their bodies from decay. However, inside the suits that have been found so far, the bodies have long since rotted away.

This is part of the autobiography of Huai Su, an 8th-century monk who was famous for his beautiful calligraphy.

PAINTING, POETRY, AND CALLIGRAPHY

To the Chinese, writing was as important for its own beauty as for the message it contained. The finest writing, or calligraphy, was done using brushes

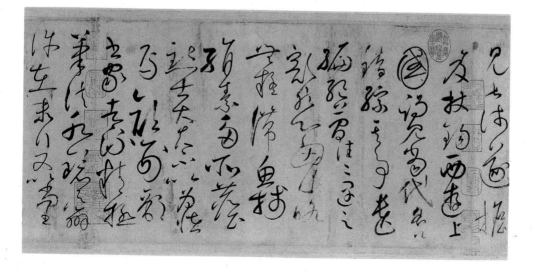

The cottage and garden at Chengdu in Sichuan province where the Tang dynasty poet Du Fu (712-770) wrote much of his poetry.

This woman flute-player is one of a group of figures of female musicians excavated from a Tang dynasty tomb. Her real-life counterpart would have entertained members of the imperial court.

dipped in ink. Painting developed from this and was done on silk, paper, and bamboo. Many paintings show scenes from court life, but others show busy streets, scenes from village life, industry, and farming. Gardens were also thought of as works of art and were favorite places for poets to sit and write, especially during the Tang dynasty. Nine hundred volumes of poetry have been collected from this period, when one of the most popular poets was Li Bai. He lived from 705 to 762 and was also famous for drinking too much rice wine. Another well-known poet from the Tang dynasty was Du Fu. He took his work so seriously that he even recommended reading poetry as a cure for malaria.

MUSIC AND DANCE

Music was a very important part of life in Imperial China. There were many different instruments including the lute, or qin, which had up to 25 strings, the harp, the flute, and a mouth organ, or sheng, made from bamboo pipes. There were also drums and bells in various sizes.

THE MONGOL INVASION

Genghis Khan proclaims himself ruler of all the Mongol tribes.

In 1206, there was an assembly of Mongol tribes in Karakorum, the capital of Mongolia. At this meeting, the various tribes appointed one supreme chief, Genghis Khan. Under Genghis Khan's leadership, the Mongols started a series of campaigns that eventually led to the establishment of the largest empire in the world at that time.

One of these campaigns began in 1211, when the Mongols invaded northern China. By 1215 they had succeeded in capturing the city of Beijing. Genghis Khan died in 1227, but his son Ögödei continued to attack the lands ruled by the Jin (see page 31). The Jin dynasty fell during the 1230s. Ögödei then turned his attentions to Europe, and by 1241 his army had stormed across Russia and on into Poland and Hungary. They turned back only when news of Ögödei's death in Karakorum finally reached them.

Ögödei was succeeded by his son Güyüg, and then by his nephew, Möngke. Möngke and his brother, Kublai Khan, planned to conquer the rest of China, but Möngke died before they could put their plan into action. Kublai Khan then became the leader of the Mongols, and in 1279 he led his armies to conquer the lands of the Southern Song. After a bitter struggle China was reunited once more, but under the leadership of a non-Chinese emperor.

A CLOSER LOOK

During the reign of Kublai Khan, all the grain that was collected as taxes was stored in huge granaries belonging to the emperor, ready for times when the harvest failed. This happened as often as every five years. Then the granaries were opened up, and the stored grain was distributed. This system was supposed to keep people from starving and ensure that farmers had enough seeds to plant for the following year. However, there were always corrupt officials, and, as a result of corruption, many died from starvation during famines.

KUBLAI KHAN

Fortunately for the Chinese, Kublai Khan was less bloodthirsty than his ancestors. Instead of destroying China and taking all its wealth, he settled there and made it the center of his vast empire, with a new capital at Beijing. He encouraged his followers to adopt a Chinese way of life and allowed people to follow any religion they wanted, including Buddhism. However, he abandoned the Chinese system of examinations for the civil service because he did not want Chinese people in all the highest government posts. He improved the road system, not only in China, but throughout the whole empire, so that his armies could move quickly when necessary. This helped to improve trade, and under his rule

A portrait of Kublai Khan (1216–1294) who founded the Yuan or Mongol dynasty in China. The Mongols called him Setsen Khan, which means "Wise Khan." He adopted many Chinese ways, but his empire outlasted him by only 74 years.

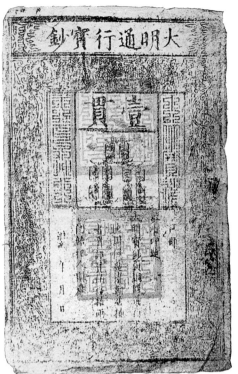

China began to flourish again. The Chinese system of paper money was used throughout the empire as a means of uniting its people, and there were provisions for looking after the sick, the orphaned, and the elderly.

Kublai Khan died in 1294. After his death, his empire began to collapse. The Mongol rulers who had followed him were weak and corrupt. The Chinese people became increasingly impatient with them. There were many revolts and uprisings and, in 1368, the Chinese finally took control of their country once more.

Paper money was already well-known in China when Kublai Khan came to power. Under his rule, it was used throughout the Mongol Empire.

A CLOSER LOOK

Europeans learned about China and the Mongol Empire from traders and travelers. Perhaps the most famous of these was the Venetian trader, Marco Polo. He set out in 1271, during the reign of Kublai Khan, and he traveled widely in Asia with his father and his uncle. On his return to Italy in 1295, Marco Polo claimed to have met Kublai Khan and to have been employed by him in various posts within the empire. His account of these travels was later published in his *Travels of Marco Polo*. In his book, Marco Polo describes the cities and people of China in great detail, but some modern-day scholars doubt whether he actually reached China.

This wooden statue of Marco Polo is from China.

TIMELINE

B.C.

*c.*551   Birth of Confucius

475   Start of Warring States period of the Zhou dynasty

247   Zheng becomes the new ruler of Qin. He will later be known as Qin Shi Huangdi.

221   Warring States period ends when the state of Qin defeats all the other states.
Qin Shi Huangdi becomes the first ruler of the Qin dynasty.

210   Death of Qin Shi Huangdi

206   Rebels led by Liu Bang defeat Qin Shi Huangdi's son.

202   After four years of struggling, Liu Bang becomes the first
emperor of the Han dynasty. His capital is at Ch'ang-an.

A.D.

1   A census taken in this year shows that there are about
57 million people living in China.

9   After a series of rebellions, a new leader, called Wang Mang,
takes control of China and brings an end to Former Han rule.

25   Wang Mang is overthrown as the Han dynasty regains control. This second
period of Han rule is known as the Later Han and has its capital at Luoyang.

220   After the leaders of the army rebel against him, the last Han emperor gives
up his throne. The empire splits into three kingdoms: Wei, Shu, and Wu.

383   Invading nomads from the north reach as far as the Yangtze River before
being defeated. China is divided into the Northern and Southern kingdoms.

581   Wendi becomes ruler of the Northern kingdom and sets out to reunite China
under the Sui dynasty.

589   China is reunited.

604   Death of Wendi. He is succeeded by his son, Yangdi.

618   Yangdi is assassinated, and the Sui dynasty is overthrown. It is
replaced by the Tang dynasty, and Ch'ang-an becomes the capital once more.

907   The Tang dynasty is defeated, and China splits up into five separate kingdoms.
In the following 53 years, five emperors try to reunite the country, but they all fail.

960   Zhao Kuang Yin becomes the first emperor of the Song dynasty.

979   China is reunited under Zhao Kuang Yin. Kaifeng becomes the capital.

1126   A tribe called the Jin overrun the northern third of China, including the
capital. One of the emperor's sons escapes to become the first emperor of
the Southern Song dynasty, based at Hangzhou.

1215   Led by Genghis Khan, the Mongols capture Beijing.

1227   Following the death of Genghis Khan, his son Ögödei
sets out to conquer all the lands in China ruled by the Jin.

1260   Kublai Khan, grandson of Genghis and nephew of Ögödei,
becomes leader of the Mongols.

1264   Kublai Khan makes Beijing into his capital
and plans to conquer the whole of China.

1271   Kublai Khan gives his dynasty the Chinese name, Yuan.

1275   Mongol armies cross the Yangtze River.

1279   The Mongols defeat the last of the Song rulers. Kublai Khan
becomes the emperor of China until his death in 1294.

GLOSSARY

acupuncture – insertion of very fine needles in specific places on the body to relieve pain and cure illnesses.

archaeologist – someone who learns about the past by studying sites, artifacts, and other objects left behind by humans.

blast furnace – a furnace into which hot air is blown to speed up the process of melting an ore.

brine – water containing a large amount of salt.

brocade – a heavy silk cloth with a raised pattern woven into it.

caravansary – a resting place in the desert for traders and their camels.

cocoon – a silky case spun by the silkworm larva to protect it while it develops into a moth.

concubine – a woman who acted as a wife to the emperor but was not married to him.

conscription – being forced to work for the emperor, usually on one of his building projects or in his army.

dynasty – a ruling family.

glaze – a liquid that is painted on to the surface of a pot after it has been shaped. It gives a smooth, shiny finish to the pot.

hemp – a plant that grows about 16 feet (5 m) tall. Fiber from the inside of the bark of its stem can be spun into yarn to make cloth.

iron foundry – the place where iron is cast, or founded, into the shape required.

kiln – a large oven in which pottery and porcelain objects are dried and hardened at very high temperatures.

lodestone – a magnetic stone, containing iron. If a piece is floated on water or suspended on a string, it points to magnetic north.

loess – a fine-grained, light-colored soil that has been carried by the wind. Good irrigation makes it very fertile.

Mongols – nomadic people who live on the vast grasslands in the north of China.

mulberry tree – a plant that was grown for its edible berries, as well as for its leaves that were used to feed silkworms.

mung bean – a bean that can either be eaten fresh or dried, or begin to grow to be eaten as bean sprouts.

nomad – someone who does not lead a settled life but moves from place to place, usually with herds of grazing sheep or cattle.

philosophy – the study of truths about reality. The search for wisdom.

polo – a game something like hockey but played on horseback.

seismograph – a machine for recording earthquakes.

soybean – a bean that is used to make both oil and flour. It is also pickled to make soy sauce.

warp – the threads that run vertically when cloth is being woven.

weft – the threads that run horizontally when cloth is being woven.

weir – a dam across a river that helps to regulate its flow and prevent flooding.

PRONUNCIATION KEY

How to Pronounce Chinese Words

```
b   d   f   g   j   k   l   m
n   p   s   t   w   y   ch  sh
```
are pronounced as they are in English

c	=	ts as in "lets"
h	=	ch as in Scottish "loch"
q	=	ch as in "chick"
x	=	sh as in "ship"
zh	=	dz as in "lads"
zh	=	j as in "jam"

a	=	ah as in "hurrah"
ai	=	ie as in "tie"
an	=	ahn as in "yon"
ao	=	ow as in "how"

e	=	oo as in "look"
ei	=	ay as in "hay"
en	=	un as in "bun"

i	=	ee as in "fee"

With other letters i sounds like y

ia	=	ya as in "yard"

o	=	aw as in "jaw"
ou	=	oe as in "toe"

u	=	oo as in "coo"

With other letters u sounds like w

ua	=	wah

Examples:

Qin = chin   Zhou = joe
Han = hahn   Xianyang = shan-yahng

FURTHER READING

Hoobler, Dorothy and Hoobler, Thomas. *Chinese Portraits.* "Images Across the Ages" series. Raintree Steck-Vaughn, Austin, TX, 1992

Lazo, Caroline. *The Terra Cotta Army of Emperor Qin.* Simon and Schuster Children's, Old Tappan, NY, 1993

Lei, Donise. *Ancient China: Its History and Culture from 2250 B.C. to A.D. 250.* Pacific Asia Press, El Monte, CA, 1992

McDonald, Fiona and Salariya, David. *Marco Polo: A Journey Through China.* Watts, Danbury, CT, 1998

Martel, Mary H. *Ancient Chinese.* Simon and Schuster Childrens, Old Tappan, NY, 1993

Odjik, Pamela. *The Chinese.* "Ancient World" series. Silver Burdett Press, Parsippany, NJ, 1991

Reese, Lyn. *The Eyes of the Empress: Women in Tang Dynasty China.* Women World CRP, Berkeley, CA, 1996

Ross, Frank, Jr. *Oracle Bones, Stars, and the Wheelbarrows: Ancient Chinese Science and Technology.* Houghton Mifflin, Boston, MA, 1990

Twist, Clint. *Marco Polo: Overland to Medieval China.* "Beyond the Horizon" series. Raintree Steck-Vaughn, Austin, TX, 1994

INDEX